Music Staff Paper FOR DUMMIES

ISBN: 978-1-4234-9585-7

HAL•LEONARD® CORPORATION

7777 W. BLUEMOUND RD. P.O. BOX 13819 MILWAUKEE, WI 53213

In Australia Contact:
Hal Leonard Australia Pty. Ltd.
4 Lentara Court
Cheltenham, Victoria, 3192 Australia
Email: ausadmin@halleonard.com.au

Visit Hal Leonard Online at
www.halleonard.com

MUSIC NOTATION GUIDE

Clefs

Treble Clef

Bass Clef

Middle C

Middle C

Notes and Rests

Whole		Half		Quarter		Eighth		Sixteenth	
Note	Rest	Note	Rest	Note	Rest	Note	Rest	Note	Rest

A dot added to a note or rest increases its value by 1/2.

Symbols

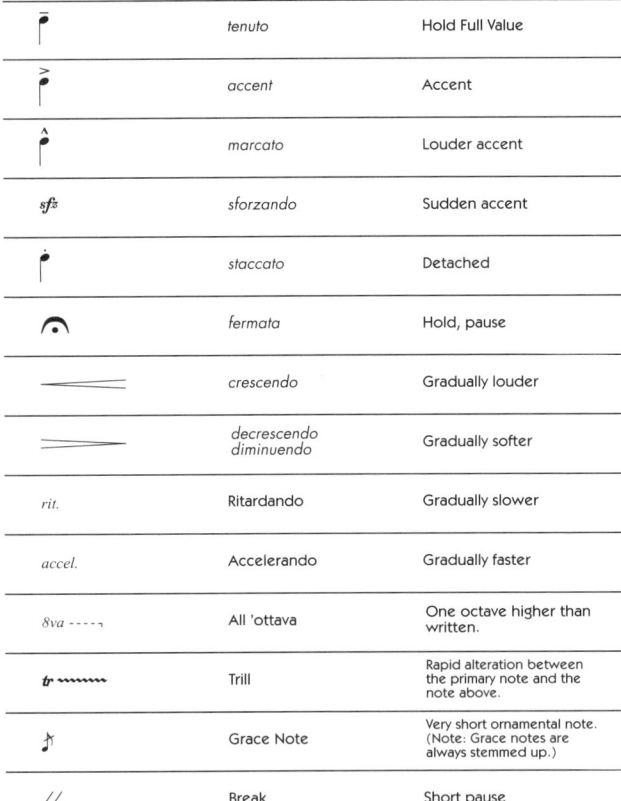

tenuto	Hold Full Value
accent	Accent
marcato	Louder accent
sforzando	Sudden accent
staccato	Detached
fermata	Hold, pause
crescendo	Gradually louder
decrescendo *diminuendo*	Gradually softer
rit.	Ritardando	Gradually slower
accel.	Accelerando	Gradually faster
8va -----	All 'ottava	One octave higher than written.
tr ﹏﹏	Trill	Rapid alteration between the primary note and the note above.
Grace Note		Very short ornamental note. (Note: Grace notes are always stemmed up.)
//	Break	Short pause

Stems and Beams

Notes below the third line are written with stems up. Notes on or above the third line are written with stems down.

Stem direction of beamed notes or chords is determined by the note farthest from the third line.

Repeat Terms and Signs

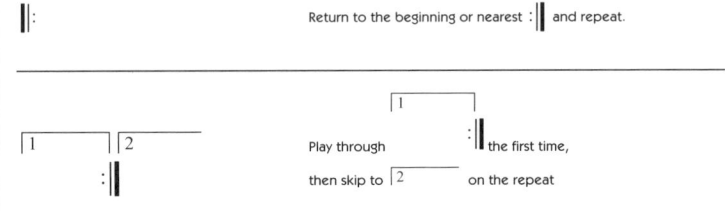

D.C. al FINE	Return to the beginning and play to Fine.
D.S. al FINE	Return to 𝄋 and play to Fine.
D.C. al CODA	Return to the beginning, play to ⊕ and skip to the Coda.
D.S. al CODA	Return to 𝄋, play to ⊕ and skip to the Coda.

Return to the beginning or nearest :‖ and repeat.

Play through ‖ the first time, then skip to ⌐2 on the repeat

Extended rest (6 measures in this example).

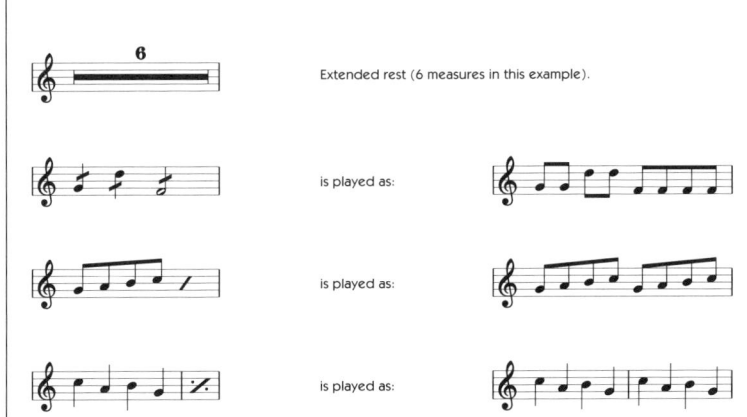

is played as:

is played as:

is played as:

is played as:

Key Signatures

Key of	C major A minor	G major E minor	D major B minor	A major F# minor	E major C# minor	B major G# minor	F# major D# minor	C# major A# minor

Order of Sharps: F – C – G – D – A – E – B

Key of	C major A minor	F major D minor	Bb major G minor	Eb major C minor	Ab major F minor	Db major Bb minor	Gb major Eb minor	Cb major Ab minor

Order of Flats: B – E – A – D – G – C – F

ORCHESTRAL INSTRUMENT RANGES AND TRANSPOSITIONS

Woodwinds

Written Range	Transposition
Piccolo	Sounds a perfect octave higher than written.
Flute	Sounds as written.
Oboe	Sounds as written.
English Horn	Sounds a perfect fifth lower than written.
B♭ Clarinet	Sounds a major second lower than written.
B♭ Bass Clarinet	Sounds a major ninth lower than written.
Bassoon	Sounds as written.
Contra Bassoon	Sounds a perfect octave lower than written.

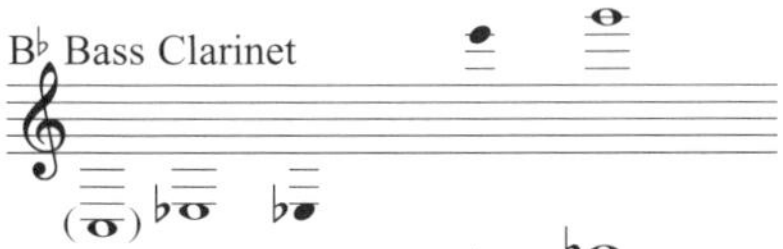

Strings

Written Range	Transposition
Violin	Sounds as written.
Viola	Sounds as written.
Violoncello	Sounds as written.
Contra Bass	Sounds a perfect octave lower than written.

Open notes indicate the extreme possible range of each instrument. Practical (commonly used) range is indicated with black notes.

Brass

Written Range	Transposition
B♭ Trumpet	Sounds a major second lower than written.
Horn in F	Sounds a perfect fifth lower than written.
Trombone	Sounds as written.
Tuba	Sounds as written.

Percussion

Written Range	Transposition
Xylophone	Sounds a perfect octave higher than written.
Marimba	Sounds as written.
Glockenspiel	Sounds two perfect octaves higher than written.
Vibraphone	Sounds as written.
Chimes	Sounds as written.
Timpani 32" 30" 29" or 28" 26" or 25" 23" 20"	Sounds as written.
Celeste	Sounds a perfect octave higher than written.
Harp	Sounds as written.
Piano	Sounds as written.

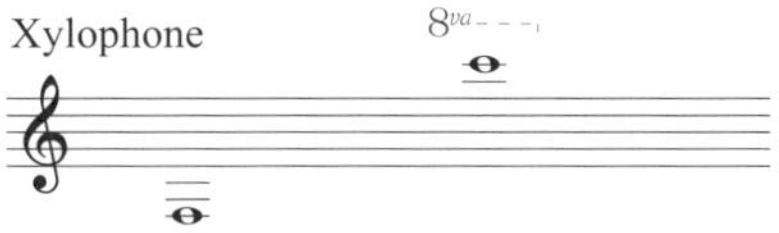

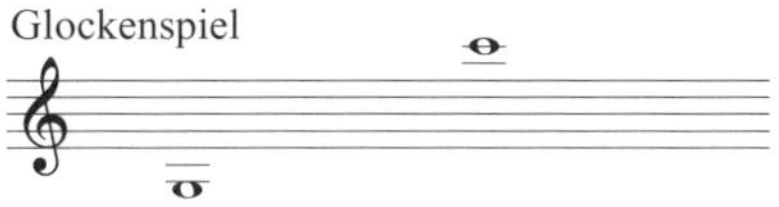

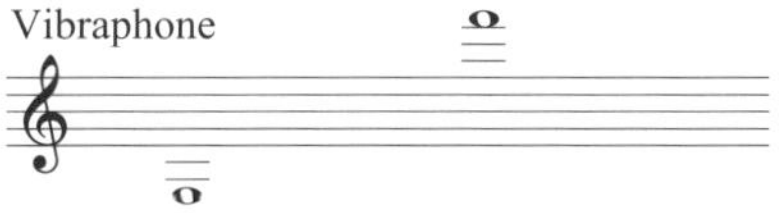

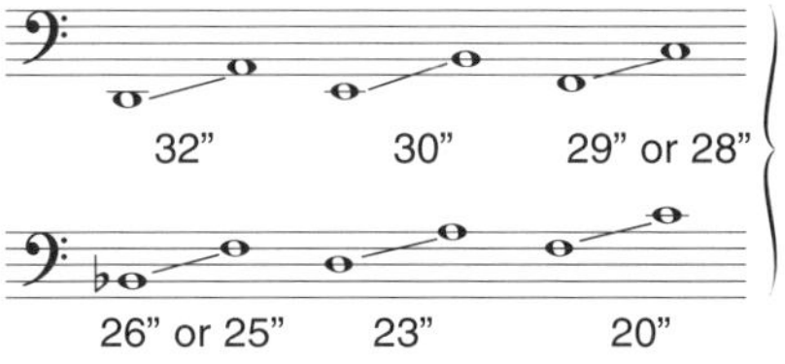

JAZZ BAND INSTRUMENT RANGES & ARTICULATIONS

Woodwinds

Written Range | Transposition

Flute — Sounds as written.

B♭ Clarinet — Sounds a major second lower than written.

E♭ Soprano Sax — Sounds a major second lower than written.

E♭ Alto Sax — Sounds a major sixth lower than written.

B♭ Tenor Sax — Sounds a major ninth lower than written.

E♭ Baritone Sax — Sounds on octave and major sixth lower than written.

Brass

Written Range | Transposition

B♭ Trumpet — Sounds a major second lower than written.

Trombone — Sounds as written.

Heavy Accent
Hold note for full time value.

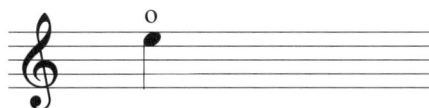

Wah
Full sound - open, not muffled.

Heavy Accent
Hold note less than full time value.

Short Gliss Up
Slide into the note from below.

Heavy Accent
Play note as short as possible.

Long Gliss Up
Slide into note from below, with longer entrance than the Short Gliss Up.

Staccato
Note is short, not heavy.

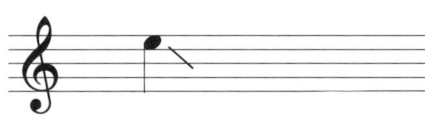

Short Gliss Down
Reverse of Short Gliss Up.

Legato Tongue
Hold note for full value.

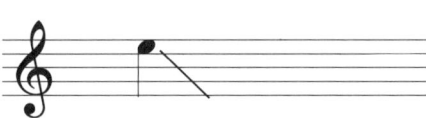

Long Gliss Down
Reverse of Long Gliss Up.

Shake
A rapid alteration between the written note and the note above.

Short Lift
Reach note using a chromatic or diatonic scale starting about a third below.

Lip Trill
Similar to a shake; done slower and with more lip control.

Long Lift
Same as Short Lift except use a longer entrance.

Flip
Sound the note, raise the pitch and drop into following note (done with lip on brass).

Short Spill
Sound note and drop rapidly using a chromatic or diatonic scale. The reverse of a Short Lift.

Smear
Slide into note from below, reaching pitch just before next note. Do not rob preceding note.

Long Spill
Same as Short Spill but with longer exit.

Doit
Note is sounded. Gliss upward from one to five notes.

Plop
Slide rapidly down harmonic or diatonic scale before sounding note.

Du
Tone is false or muffled.

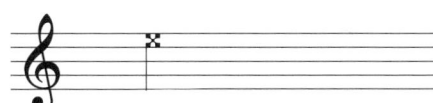

IndefiniteSound - "Ghost Note"
Deaden the tone - indefinite pitch.

GUITAR NOTATION LEGEND

Guitar music can be notated three different ways: on a *musical staff*, in *tablature*, and in *rhythm slashes*.

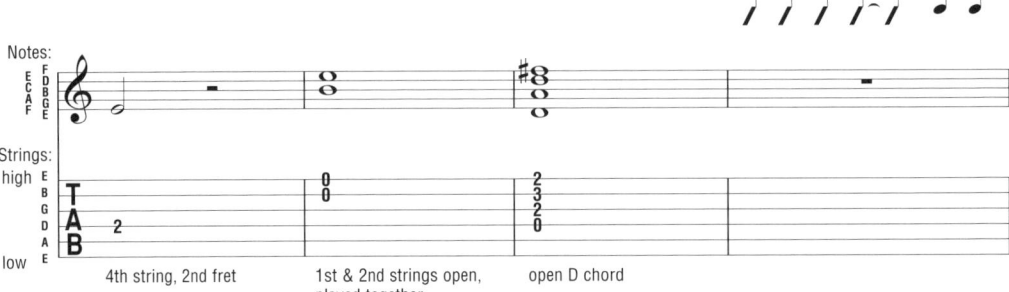

RHYTHM SLASHES are written above the staff. Strum chords in the rhythm indicated. Use the chord diagrams found at the top of the first page of the transcription for the appropriate chord voicings. Round noteheads indicate single notes.

THE MUSICAL STAFF shows pitches and rhythms and is divided by bar lines into measures. Pitches are named after the first seven letters of the alphabet.

TABLATURE graphically represents the guitar fingerboard. Each horizontal line represents a string, and each number represents a fret.

4th string, 2nd fret   1st & 2nd strings open, played together   open D chord

HALF-STEP BEND: Strike the note and bend up 1/2 step.

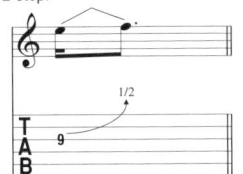

WHOLE-STEP BEND: Strike the note and bend up one step.

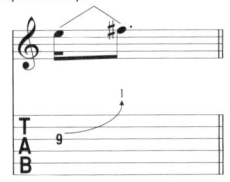

GRACE NOTE BEND: Strike the note and immediately bend up as indicated.

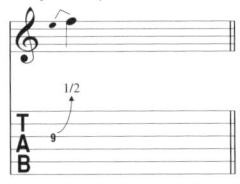

SLIGHT (MICROTONE) BEND: Strike the note and bend up 1/4 step.

BEND AND RELEASE: Strike the note and bend up as indicated, then release back to the original note. Only the first note is struck.

PRE-BEND: Bend the note as indicated, then strike it.

VIBRATO: The string is vibrated by rapidly bending and releasing the note with the fretting hand.

WIDE VIBRATO: The pitch is varied to a greater degree by vibrating with the fretting hand.

HAMMER-ON: Strike the first (lower) note with one finger, then sound the higher note (on the same string) with another finger by fretting it without picking.

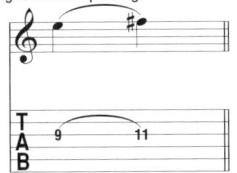

PULL-OFF: Place both fingers on the notes to be sounded. Strike the first note and without picking, pull the finger off to sound the second (lower) note.

LEGATO SLIDE: Strike the first note and then slide the same fret-hand finger up or down to the second note. The second note is not struck.

SHIFT SLIDE: Same as legato slide, except the second note is struck.

TRILL: Very rapidly alternate between the notes indicated by continuously hammering on and pulling off.

TAPPING: Hammer ("tap") the fret indicated with the pick-hand index or middle finger and pull off to the note fretted by the fret hand.

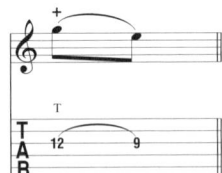

NATURAL HARMONIC: Strike the note while the fret-hand lightly touches the string directly over the fret indicated.

PINCH HARMONIC: The note is fretted normally and a harmonic is produced by adding the edge of the thumb or the tip of the index finger of the pick hand to the normal pick attack.

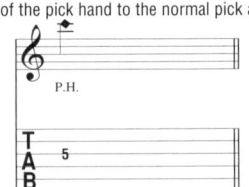

PICK SCRAPE: The edge of the pick is rubbed down (or up) the string, producing a scratchy sound.

MUFFLED STRINGS: A percussive sound is produced by laying the fret hand across the string(s) without depressing, and striking them with the pick hand.

PALM MUTING: The note is partially muted by the pick hand lightly touching the string(s) just before the bridge.

RAKE: Drag the pick across the strings indicated with a single motion.

TREMOLO PICKING: The note is picked as rapidly and continuously as possible.

VIBRATO BAR DIVE AND RETURN: The pitch of the note or chord is dropped a specified number of steps (in rhythm), then returned to the original pitch.

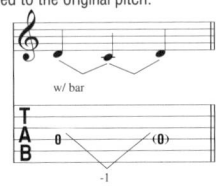

VIBRATO BAR SCOOP: Depress the bar just before striking the note, then quickly release the bar.

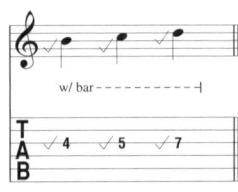

VIBRATO BAR DIP: Strike the note and then immediately drop a specified number of steps, then release back to the original pitch.

BASS NOTATION LEGEND

Bass music can be notated two different ways: on a *musical staff*, and in *tablature*.

THE MUSICAL STAFF shows pitches and rhythms and is divided by bar lines into measures. Pitches are named after the first seven letters of the alphabet.

TABLATURE graphically represents the bass fingerboard. Each horizontal line represents a string, and each number represents a fret.

Notes:

3rd string, open   2nd string, 2nd fret   1st & 2nd strings open, played together

HAMMER-ON: Strike the first (lower) note with one finger, then sound the higher note (on the same string) with another finger by fretting it without picking.

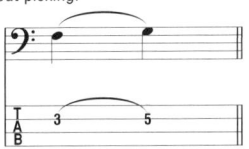

PULL-OFF: Place both fingers on the notes to be sounded. Strike the first note and without picking, pull the finger off to sound the second (lower) note.

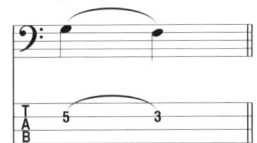

LEGATO SLIDE: Strike the first note and then slide the same fret-hand finger up or down to the second note. The second note is not struck.

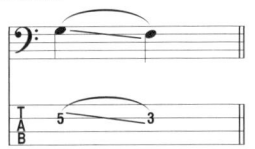

SHIFT SLIDE: Same as legato slide, except the second note is struck.

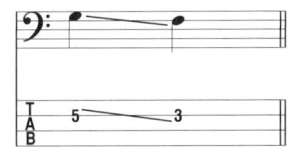

TRILL: Very rapidly alternate between the notes indicated by continuously hammering on and pulling off.

TREMOLO PICKING: The note is picked as rapidly and continuously as possible.

VIBRATO: The string is vibrated by rapidly bending and releasing the note with the fretting hand.

SHAKE: Using one finger, rapidly alternate between two notes on one string by sliding either a half-step above or below.

NATURAL HARMONIC: Strike the note while the fret hand lightly touches the string directly over the fret indicated.

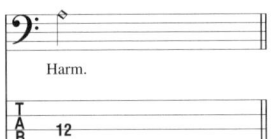

MUFFLED STRINGS: A percussive sound is produced by laying the fret hand across the string(s) without depressing them and striking them with the pick hand.

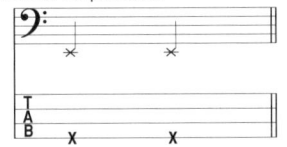

BEND: Strike the note and bend up the interval shown.

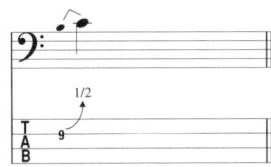

BEND AND RELEASE: Strike the note and bend up as indicated, then release back to the original note. Only the first note is struck.

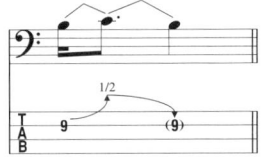

RIGHT-HAND TAP: Hammer ("tap") the fret indicated with the "pick-hand" index or middle finger and pull off to the note fretted by the fret hand.

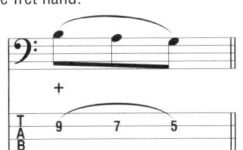

LEFT-HAND TAP: Hammer ("tap") the fret indicated with the "fret-hand" index or middle finger.

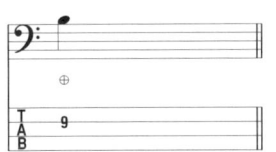

SLAP: Strike ("slap") string with right-hand thumb.

POP: Snap ("pop") string with right-hand index or middle finger.

Additional Musical Definitions

(accent) • Accentuate note (play it louder).

(accent) • Accentuate note with great intensity.

(staccato) • Play the note short.

  • Downstroke

V • Upstroke

D.S. al Coda • Go back to the sign (%), then play until the measure marked "*To Coda*," then skip to the section labelled "Coda."

D.C. al Fine • Go back to the beginning of the song and play until the measure marked "*Fine*" (end).

Bass Fig. • Label used to recall a recurring pattern.

Fill • Label used to identify a brief melodic figure which is to be inserted into the arrangement.

tacet • Instrument is silent (drops out).

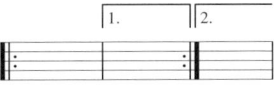

  • Repeat measures between signs.

  • When a repeated section has different endings, play the first ending only the first time and the second ending only the second time.

NOTE: Tablature numbers in parentheses mean:
  1. The note is being sustained over a system (note in standard notation is tied), or
  2. The note is sustained, but a new articulation (such as a hammer-on, pull-off, slide or vibrato) begins.

DRUM NOTATION LEGEND

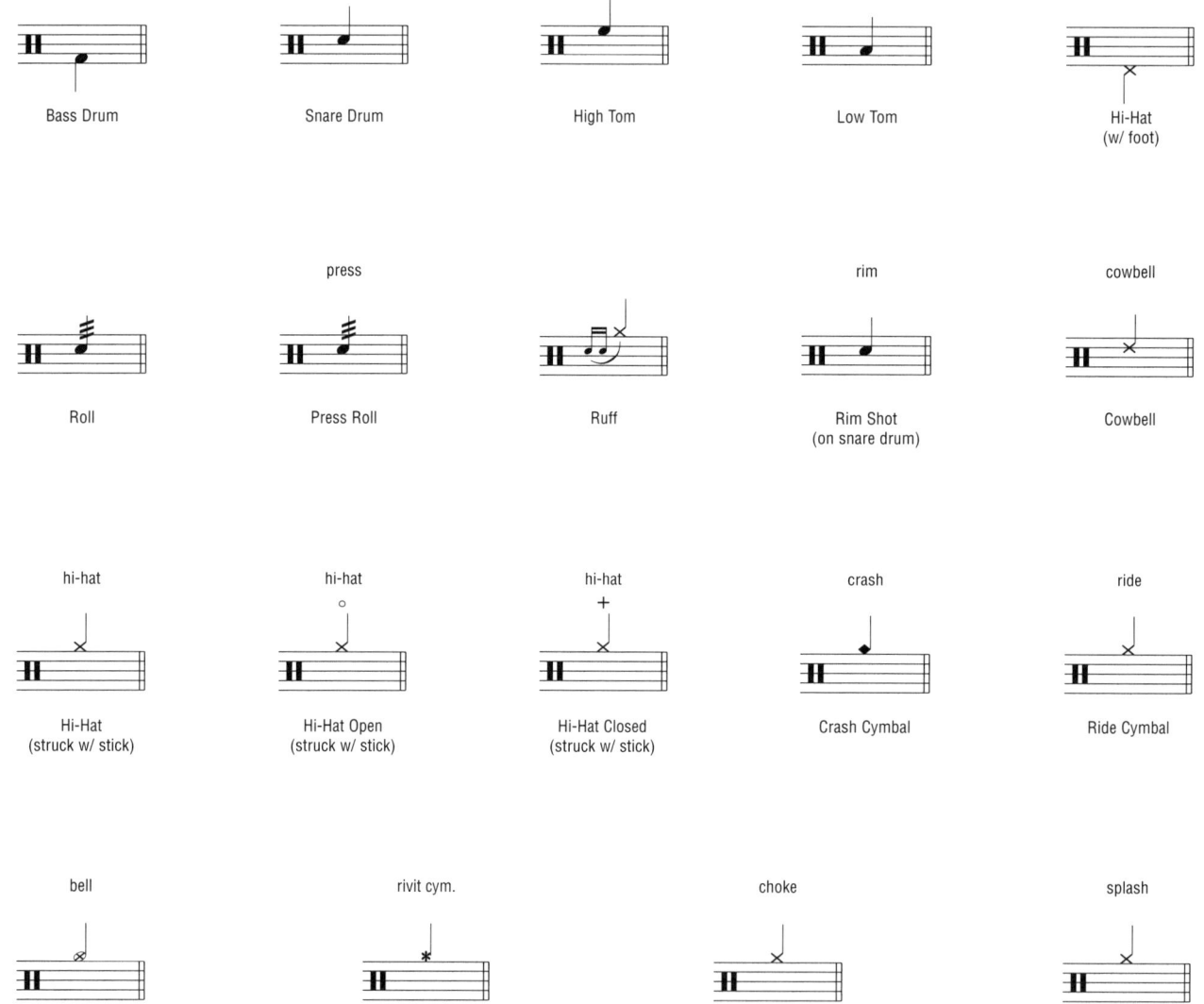

| Bass Drum | Snare Drum | High Tom | Low Tom | Hi-Hat (w/ foot) |

| Roll | press Press Roll | Ruff | rim Rim Shot (on snare drum) | cowbell Cowbell |

| hi-hat Hi-Hat (struck w/ stick) | hi-hat Hi-Hat Open (struck w/ stick) | hi-hat Hi-Hat Closed (struck w/ stick) | crash Crash Cymbal | ride Ride Cymbal |

| bell Cymbal Bell | rivit cym. Rivit Cymbal | choke Dampen Cymbal | splash Splash Cymbal |

HAL•LEONARD®